Media-ted Virus Debate

When an African President Questioned Cause of AIDS

Jacob J Akol

(Abridged from MA in Communications Thesis
Validated by the University of Leeds.
February 2001, Oxford Centre for Mission Studies)

Africa
World Books
Pty Ltd

Abbreviations

AIDS	Acquired Immune Deficiency Syndrome
ANC	African National Congress
AFP	Agence France-Press
AP	Associated Press
BBC	British Broadcasting Corporation
Cosatu	Congress of South African Trade Unions.
CNN	Cable News Network
EB	Encyclopaedia Britannica
HIV	Human Immunodeficiency Virus
JAMA	Journal of American Medical Association
NBC	National Broadcasting Company
NGOs	Non-Governmental Organisations
STD	Sexually Transmitted Diseases
UNAIDS	United Nations Programme on AIDS
UK	United Kingdom
USA	United States of America
UN	United Nations
WHO	World Health Organisation

Terminology

African AIDS refers to AIDS resulting from the HIV strains commonly found in Africa and which are generally transmitted through heterosexual intercourse.

African media [am] normally refers to media organisations based in Africa.

African media in Diaspora [amd] refers to media organisations that are based outside Africa but are concerned with African issues.

Dissident Media [dm] refers to the media used by dissident scientists or those media organisations that exist solely for the advocacy of dissidents' views.

Dissident Scientists refers to the scientists who argue that "HIV is not the cause of AIDS".

Fringe media [fm] is any media that does not fit into the category "mainstream media".

HIV positive/negative refers to those infected with the virus as "positive" while those free of the virus "negative".

Mainstream media [mm] refers to those media, which can be reasonably described as major national, regional and international dailies, weeklies and monthlies. These will include major news agencies such as Reuters, AP and AFP. They are normally part of the establishment and generally supportive of the dominant ideological views.

Mainstream Scientists refers to the scientists who believe that HIV is the cause of AIDS.

Western media [wm] refers to any mass media organisation generally owned and residing in North America, Western Europe or Australia.

White South African media [wsm] refers to the distinct South African media which is generally regarded by South African blacks as being more reflective and protective of white South Africans and Western values than of black Africans in general and black South Africans in particular.

List of Contents

Preamble

By the mid 1990s, Western media interest in HIV/AIDS activities had waned because forecasts of a high rise in HIV infections and AIDS deaths in the wealthier parts of the world did not materialise. Prevention programmes were successful while drug treatment was delaying the on-set of AIDS.

Africa was different. HIV infections were rising rapidly and evenly among the sexes. AIDS deaths were also increasing while African leadership appeared to be in denial of the disease. Ignorance about the disease prevailed while any government prevention programmes were poorly financed and organised. Still the media paid scant attention to what was clearly an epidemic by the turn of the century.

UNAIDS planned to hold the 13th International AIDS Conference in Durban, South Africa, in 2000, hoping to attract the attention of the wealthier world. It got more media coverage than it bargained for: An old debate among scientist turned political when the host-country's president unexpectedly intervened in apparent support of dissident scientists' views; controversy followed and the media poured in. Controversial issues on HIV/AIDS made headlines and kept African AIDS in the news throughout 2000. How did the media conduct itself in such debates – which at times had racial undertones - and with what likely effect on the HIV/AIDS programme in Africa?

Who Cares?

HIV/AIDS was and still is currently a serious threat to Africa, with the highest rate of infections and deaths from the disease. With no cure or vaccine yet available, the epidemic is most likely to worsen; and controversies and debates are bound to increase around the disease. An analytical study, focusing on the role of the media in the on-going debate, is, therefore, bound to be of considerable interest to the parties involved in the debate; to the NGOs, Church organisations, as well as families and individuals involved in the care of the HIV/AIDS victims. It should be of interest to governments, people living with HIV-AIDS and practically anyone who cares to know how the mass media addresses itself to serious issues, such as the HIV-AIDS epidemic in Africa. Findings and conclusions from this research could be instructive to those who are new to the on-going HIV-AIDS debate, its threat to the world in general and to Africa in particular.

Introduction

What Prizes the Durban Conference?

The first phenomenon was that some 1,500 media correspondents turned up at the 13th International Aids Conference in Durban, South Africa, in July 2000, arguably a record for an international event taking place in Africa. Sustained local and international media coverage of the AIDS epidemic in Africa had started earlier in the year and was continued long after the conference. African AIDS was a headline in some of the leading national and international media. But, this cannot be fully explained by increased news value arising out of the ever-increasing HIV infections and AIDS deaths in Africa nor by controversies rekindled by then South African President.

The second was the seemingly increasing polarisation within the news media, whereby a rigid line seemed to manifest itself between the mainstream media and the fringe media, particularly in the coverage of the AIDS epidemic in Africa. The mainstream media appeared to be largely uncritical of the methods used, the data and views presented to them by mainstream scientists and AIDS organisations while at the same time it appeared to be overwhelmingly critical of the dissident scientists and their sympathisers - such as then South African President.

On the other hand the fringe media appeared to be totally uncritical of the views of the dissidents and their sympathisers like Mbeki and extremely critical of mainstream scientists and media. Marxist theorists could explain the mainstream media behaviour as typical of a bourgeoisie media committed to defending hegemony of capitalism over other systems while Commercial Laissez-Faire theorists would see the behaviour of the fringe media as typically rebellious of authority and expressing anti-capitalism, democracy and freedom of the individual. However, these alone would not account for the seemingly heightened emotions with which opinions were expressed on both sides of the media.

The third occurrence was that an unusually large number of top international research scientists attended the conference, most likely because they expected heavy media presence at the conference. This may be explained by the theory, which argues that when it comes to looking for research funding, facts do not speak for themselves any more. "Selling science" in the popular press has become the key to guarantying private and public funding for research. It could also be speculated that AIDS conferences have come to resample pseudo or political events more than scientific events.

The hypothesis is that in addition to the above, a fuller explanation for all the three occurrences must include:

The South African historical background, its current cultural, racial, and social make up, where the very rich - mostly whites - and the very poor - mostly blacks - are struggling to co-exist peacefully in a country where political power is largely in the hands of black South Africans while economic power is largely in the hands of white South Africans;

Overrating of President Mbeki's influence, both in South Africa and the African region, may fully explain the obsession of both the media and the debating parties with Mbeki's ideas.

The Mbeki Factor

The ten months period leading to the 13th International AIDS Conference held in Durban, South Africa, from 9th to 14th July 2000, and the five months that followed, were characterised by intense arguments in the media on issues of considerable controversy and significance to the world in general and Africa in particular. These arguments emanated from what was described as "an old myth" (UNAIDS, 2000:1) and "conspiracy theories surrounding the disease" of AIDS.

These issues were sparked off by a series of views and actions by then host country's leader, President Thabo Mbeki. His views included the now widely publicised doubts about the generally accepted view that HIV is the cause of AIDS. Mbeki has argued that AIDS, being a syndrome of more than 30 diseases, could not possibly be caused by a single virus and that poverty may indeed be the main factor (Mbeki, July 9, 2000) in the possible causes of AIDS in Africa.

However, the key controversial issue centred on his decision to invite some well-known dissident scientists to discuss issues which mainstream scientists had believed were settled a long time ago.

The media found these controversial arguments on HIV/AIDS issues irresistible. HIV/AIDS issues in general and its epidemic proportions in Africa in particular, became headline news throughout 2000 in some of the best-known mainstream international, regional and national media outlets. Then UNAIDS boss Dr Peter Piot, is on record as saying: "Before this, (Daily Mail & Guardian, July 16, 2000), when did the AIDS conference make the front pages of the *New York Times* and *Washington Post?*"

A recurrent question, which much of the mainstream media had been asking, was the source of Mbeki's information that had turned "an excellent president into "a loon" (Plotz, July 14 2000). The media zeroed in on an off the cuff remark by one of President Mbeki's aides that the president was a devoted "web surfer" and they concluded from that that he had obtained his information from the Internet - specifically from the dissident scientists Web site.

AIDS Victims

While these issues were being publicly debated, the man and woman in the street, the HIV positive mother-to-be, the AIDS patient receiving treatment or not with retroviral drugs, the mourner at the graveyard and the AIDS orphan must have been terribly confused by the conflicting messages from those they look to for answers. This must raise serious ethical and moral questions for the scientific and medical professional, the politician, the drug manufacturer, the aid worker, the clergy, and last but not least the media professional.

The thesis relates a seemingly persistent and dividing ideological line within the media to the relevant media theories concerning news and news events. It is hoped it will shed some light on the rationale behind the various choices that must be made by various media professionals within the news chain to satisfy established ideological lines. The thesis proposes that these ideological divisions contribute to the way HIV/AIDS issues were reported.

The study is also concerned with the importance of ethics and morality within the news reporting of the disease. It raises ethical and moral questions where actions, more than words, are required for the care of those infected with the virus or dying from AIDS. It asks questions concerning ethical and moral justification for single-minded pursuit of truth, as is claimed to be the case by those involved on both sides of the debate.

What is HIV/AIDS?

The Encyclopaedia Britannica defines AIDS as "a fatal transmission disorder of immune system that is caused by the human immunodeficiency virus (HIV). In most cases (EB, 1997) HIV slowly attacks and destroys the immune system, the body's defence against disease, leaving the infected individual vulnerable to malignancies and infections that eventually cause death. AIDS is the last stage of HIV infection, during which time these diseases arise."

HIV is believed to have been "isolated in 1983, and by 1985 (EB, ibid.) serologic tests to detect the virus had been developed". But there is, as yet, no vaccine or cure against HIV infections, though a number of retroviral drugs are believed to slow the development of AIDS in individuals infected with HIV and also reduce mother to child transmission of the virus. "Efforts at prevention (EB, ibid.) have been focused primarily on changes in sexual behaviour such as abstinence, monogamy, the use of barrier contraceptives and other 'safe sex' methods".

The Duesberg Connection

The widely accepted concept that HIV is the cause of AIDS was first challenged by Dr Peter Duesberg, a retro virologist at the University of California, Berkeley, "who in 1987 (Science, 1994) published a paper arguing that HIV is harmless" and had gone on to argue that "factors such as illicit drug use and AZT, the anti-HIV compound, actually cause the disease".

For a while, his views received attention from scientific journals and the mainstream media. But, as he continued to fire off more and more challenges and accusations of corruption and conspiracy within the AIDS establishment, his views, and those of his colleagues in the USA, Canada, Europe and Australia, were largely ignored by the mainstream scientists and scientific publications as well as by the mainstream media. Only the fringe and dissident media, such as Duesberg's own website, continued to publicise their views.

What is News?

Any news apprentice will be told that "news is something unusual, something which stands out", a concept usually illustrated in Western journalism by the notion that "when a dog bites a man, that is not news; but when a man bites a dog, that is news". "This seemingly obvious formula (Ginneken, 1998:31) presupposes a particular world view", for there are indeed other cultures and societies where dogs are eaten, i.e. China, (Ginneken, ibid.) and presumably biting one would not be such big news after all.

▌ Ginneken (1998, ibid.) subscribes to the view that "news is inherently ideological - by its very nature". The "facts", as defined by each media organisation, "are emphasised, but the underlying ideology remains disguised." Ginneken (1998, ibid.31-32) points out that news is "like the proverbial iceberg: a brilliant and impressive 10 percent of its mass is visible above the water line, a dark and treacherous 90 percent remains invisible under water". He warns that "those who let themselves be attracted and dazzled by the former, may be shipwrecked and sunk by the latter".

▌ News is also defined as a social institution that is meaningless unless it relates "to other institutions and discourses (Hartly, 1982:9) operating at the same time, and the people making the news have to fit their activities into a complex social network". Media organisations, therefore, have to negotiate their interests with those of others to which their fortunes are intricately linked and could be in opposition. This reality, Hartly argues, constrains "the choices open to journalists and broadcasters". Still, "the news is, inevitably, what they say it is. Hence much of the critical attention given to news organisation concentrates on watching the watchdog. Otherwise we would have no independent confirmation that what sounds so credible and natural in the news is actually right".

▌ Cohen and Young (1973:15) have argued that "news is not," as the "dominant Commercial-Laissez-Faire picture of the media" perceives it, "an objective body of events which occur and which the journalist pursues, captures in his notebook or newsreel and takes back triumphantly to his editor". According to this view, "News, rather, is manufactured by journalists (Cohen & Young, ibid.:97) through interpreting and selecting events to fit pre-existing categories, themselves a product of bureaucratic exigencies of news organisations ...". This, they argue, is not the sort of control one finds in totalitarian states:

> To stress this creative nature of journalism (Cohen & Young, ibid.) is not to imply a Mass Manipulative model: distortion is not limited to the heavy hand of direct censorship but is a less obvious process - often unconscious and unstated - of interpreting the event in terms of an acceptable world view.

Robert Cirino (Cohen & Young, ibid.:16), "whose case is that the American news media use bias, distortion and censorship to manipulate public opinion", asserts that "the journalist does not merely make an inspired guess about potential interest of an item. Powerful commercial and political interests direct his attention to particular issues while shutting out his awareness of others." He (Cirino, 1971) warned that

> We the public should be aware that many decisions are made by editors who select news in a way designed to support certain view-points, to be entertaining at the expense of 'hard' reality or not to antagonise the audience. Regardless of which reason, the bias that results is one that favours conservative viewpoints and the status quo.

▌ Daniel Boorstin (Tumber, 1999:16) would most likely classify the biennial international Aids conferences as a "pseudo-event" because it has many of the following characteristics he associates with pseudo-events:

> It is planted primarily (not always exclusively) for the immediate purpose of being reported or reproduced. Its occurrence is arranged for the convenience of the reporting or reproducing media. Its

success is measured by how widely it is reported. Time relations in
it are commonly fictitious or factitious; the announcement is given
out in advance 'for future release' and written as if the event had
occurred in the past. The question, 'Is it real?' is less important than
'Is it newsworthy?' Its relations to the underlying reality of the situation is ambiguous. Its interest arises largely from this very ambiguity... Without some of this ambiguity a pseudo-event cannot be
very interesting.

It is Boorstin's view that "In recent years, (Tumber, ibid:17) successful politicians have been those most adept at using the press and other means to create
pseudo-events" that they call 'facts' - "while editorial writers were simply
expressing opinions".

Boorstin's (Tumber, ibid.) other characteristic of pseudo-events is the use of
the interview to create 'pseudo-news'. "By the interview technique", journalists
will incite public figures "to make statements which will sound like news". This
technique, he argued, "has grown into a devious apparatus which, in skilful
hands, can shape a national policy."

Another important Boorstin view associated with the pseudo-event theory
is the development of the news 'leak', which he believes "is now one of the main
vehicles for communicating important information from officials to the public".

▌ In his essay (Tumber, 1999:103), Mark Fishman turns his attention to the
practice of "the beat" in news reporting. It is a journalistic concept "grounded
in the actual working world of reporters". It has advantages and disadvantages.
Reporters get to know the newsmakers of "the beat" area well and the news from
such sources would normally be treated by desk editors as "facts" and "reliable",
ensuring fewer controversies or law suits. On the other hand, reporters often
become too attached to "the beat" and the newsmakers of the territory. Fishman
(Tumber, ibid.:110) argues that:

Reporters follow rounds which expose them only to bureaucratically
produced accounts, and they apply agency schemes of interpretation

and relevance to the accounts. By doing so, the reporter makes the
successive levels of bureaucratic account production the foundation
for a news story. A journalist can change the sources upon which a
story is based simply by shifting the emphasis of what the story will
be about.

This is important, because HIV/AIDS institutions have become permanent
and good sources of regular and important news so much that it requires "beat"
reporters from news organisations. These journalists become the highly valued
"experts" of media organisations.

▌ Also in their essay (in Tumber, 1999:25) Johan Galtung and Mari Holmboe
Ruge listed four important western culture-bound factors influencing the
transition from events to news:

> The more the event concerns elite nations, the more probable that it
> will become a news item. The more the event concerns elite people,
> the more probable that it will become a news item. The more the
> event can be seen in personal terms, as due to the actions of specific
> individuals the more probable that it will become a news item. The
> more negative the event in its consequences the more probable it will
> become a news item.

▌ News is simplified and dramatised to maximise entertainment and to
retain vast audience's attention for the advertising industry. Actual facts and
truth are often the victims. "Especially in America, we like to think of things in
terms of good guys and bad guys," said former foreign correspondent for AP,
ABC, and *The New York Times*, Malcolm Browne:

> If one of the partners in a conflict is one that most people can identify
> with as a good guy, then you've got a situation in which it's possible to
> root for the home team (Moeller, 1999:13-14). That's what a lot of
> news is about. We love to see everything in terms of black and white,

right and wrong, truths versus lies. We do mislead. We have to use symbolism. Symbolism is a useful psychological tool, but it can be terribly misused. It can be misleading. It can lead to great cruelty and injustice, but all those things are components of entertainment".

▌ Scientific events are "shows" comparable to the Hollywood Academy Awards or Olympic Gold Medals. "Each year (Nelkin, 1995:15) the media devotes considerable attention to winners of the Nobel Prize." They use "language recycled from reports of the Olympic Games: 'Another strong US show'; 'Americans again this year receive a healthy share of the Nobel Prizes'; 'US showed it is doing something right by scoring a near sweep of the Prize'; The winning American style.'"

▌ Aids was ignored for a long time by the mainstream media because it was the disease of minorities such as "gays" and "drug users" (Nelkkin, 1995:103). Mainstream media interest was aroused occasionally at such times as when "Dr. Anthony Fauci raised the possibility that AIDS might be transmissible to the entire population through routine close contact (Nelkin, 1995:101-102). To the media this suggested that everyone was at risk."

▌ Aids, however, remained a disease for 'others': "Africans, Haitians, those who are somehow immoral," (Nelkin, ibid.) so it was hardly of interest to the mainstream media.

▌ Nelkin (95:119) also noted the dependency of science journalists on what is handed to them by scientific organisations:

> The complexity and uncertainties of scientific subject matter reinforce the tendency of journalists to rely on press releases, press conferences and other pre-packaged sources of information. Journalists attempt to compensate for the inadequacies of their own judgement by cultivating scientists who will give them a "scoop". But as historian Anthony Smith suggests, "One man's scoop is frequently another's carefully camouflaged handout."

❚ Moemeka and Kasoma (Kasoma, 1994:38) have proposed an approach to journalism based on African traditional ethics and morality. Their views are important because they take note of the seeming contradictions between what they propose and the Western approach to journalism. (Referred to in Conclusion)

Reaction of the News Media

The thesis argues that Mbeki's views on HIV/AIDS, the dissident scientists' open arms-embracing of Mbeki and the mainstream scientists' negative reaction to this "marriage of convenience", were simply very good news for news media. Mbeki's venture into the world of the HIV/AIDS debate merely provided a fertile ground for the manufacture of a variety of news reports, feature articles, analytical opinion pieces and general drama and entertainment.

The 13th International Aids Conference in Durban, South Africa, was therefore expected to be a very unusual media event. Some of the main reasons were clearly those events preceding the conference. Also the UNAIDS series of press releases (23 listed from January - June 2000), announcing the ever increasing number of HIV infections, AIDS deaths and a very bleak future it painted for sub-Sahara Africa in general and for South Africa in particular, a nation "which now (UNAIDS, June, 2000) has 4.2 million people living with HIV/ AIDS, the highest number in the world".

Add South Africa's own multicultural/multiracial environment: a country which had recently emerged from extreme racial conflict and is still struggling to reconcile disparity between the very wealthy few - mostly whites - and the very poor majority - mostly blacks; a Nelson Mandela's country, himself then a living legend the media could not resist comparing with Mbeki. All these provided the ideal stage for the tragedy of the African AIDS drama to unfold; a drama that no media organisation or foreign correspondent would wish to miss.

It seemed that by January 2000 President Mbeki's life and that of the South African society was ripe for the picking. The AIDS issue and the conference provided both the stage and the battlefield. Mbeki's interactions with those who questioned his views were largely interpreted in confrontational and negative terms. For the mainstream media, it seemed just like old time western movies: "Good Guys" or mainstreamers versus "Bad Guys" or dissenters. Key battlefield phrases and words, such as: challenge, attack, fight, battle, war, row, take on, central stage, dig in, accuse, anger, tackle, slam, warning, ground zero, fallout, uproar, scale down, retreat, mad... were used liberally.

The inevitable questions began to fly from the media: Where did Mbeki get his information about HIV-AIDS from? Is Mbeki resorting to the racial card? Is South Africa's racial harmony coming apart? Are Mandela's shoes too big for Mbeki? Why is he behaving like Robert Mugabe of Zimbabwe? Has he got AIDS himself and he's in denial like the rest of his fellow Africans? Is he becoming sensitive to criticism from political opposition? Is he concentrating power in the presidency for himself? Are his ministers really loyal or are they afraid of him? Is there unity in Mbeki's party on this and that? Why is there not enough investment coming to South Africa? Where is his "African Renaissance" philosophy heading? How long can Mbeki hold South Africa together? Is he a wise man or a fool? Is he mad or sane?

Note how the HIV/AIDS epidemic has faded into the background in these questions as related political issues took central stage. From here on, media reports concentrated more on the politics of HIV/AIDS rather than on the science and the effect of the disease on Africa.

For the mainstream media the answers provided to these questions, either by the writers themselves or by those they chose for comment, appear to be in most cases overwhelmingly negative of Mbeki's and dissidents' views or highly pessimistic about the future of Africa in general and of South Africa in particular. For the dissidents' and fringe media, the opposite appears to be the case.

But, no matter how one looks at it, media coverage of HIV/AIDS in Africa in 2000 was dominated by the views and actions of the South African President. In no way could justice be done to any review of the media role on the continent over that period without full consideration of Mbeki's views and their attraction for the media.

Mainstream White South African Media [mwsam]

On Mbeki
Some key adjectival words and phrases used by this media: *ill-informed, misled, confused, naïve, racist, rush, fanatical, obsessed, irrational, incompetent, intolerant,*

unsympathetic, uncharitable, cruel, heartless, combative, grandiose and ill-conceived
ideas, dictatorial or undemocratic tendencies, unwise, mad . . .

It is perhaps important to take note of the background in which media discourse in HIV/AIDS issues took place in South Africa, where the mainstream media see President Mbeki's views as closely linked to, if not inseparable from, those of the dissident scientists. This should help us understand how the black leadership perceived criticism of Mbeki, no matter how legitimate, from the mainstream white South African media. Earlier, much of the white South African media [wsam] - which dominates in South Africa - was accused of portraying the country's black leaders, "notably President Thabo Mbeki, (Roberts, 2000), as corrupt, anti democratic and dictatorial, the ANC charged at a hearing into racism in the media." Only former president, Nelson Mandela, argued the ANC, was spared from criticism by the white media. An ANC spokesman is quoted in a reference to the white media:

What is remarkable about the pieces of unashamedly racist journalism we have cited (Roberts, ibid.) is that they do not go further
to portray Mbeki as a criminal and an HIV-positive rapist of white
women. Six years after the end of white minority rule, many journalists still carried 'in their heads at all times the stereotype of
blacks as amoral, violent, disrespectful of private property, incapable
of refinement through education and driven by hereditary satanic
impulses. The white media measure Mandela's success against his
ability to allay white fears, and eventually proclaimed him as excep-
tional to the rest of South Africa's black leaders.

Looking at the coverage by the largest and most influential white South African news publication, the *Daily Mail & Guardian* [wsam], only three out of 30 articles randomly retrieved from their website were clearly favourable to Mbeki and the dissidents views. The rest could be interpreted by Mbeki's government, dissident scientists and sympathising media as offensive, dramatic or alarmist.

Using metaphors, David Le Page (*Daily Mail & Guardian*, March 14, 2000), for example, reported that "AIDS has attacked the intellectual resources of the body politics as successfully as it has assaulted the immune systems of many South Africans". There appeared to be a "profound misunderstanding on the part of the president, successive health ministers and their immediate advisers of the nature of science, how it advances and how to make use of its insights."

There was "disregard for science and scientists" by Mbeki and according to "Mark Heywood of the Aids Law Project, 'they are looking for shortcuts, and therefore willing to rubbish the views of the scientific community'". The article concluded that the government was looking for "particular answers from the Aids problem. Accustomed to political answers that can be negotiated and economic answers that can be argued till the cows come home, it is affronted when science cannot play."

Although it could be argued that there is a lot of truth in this article, the nature of South African social, cultural, racial and historical background would make Le Page's views disagreeable to Mbeki and his supporters who would dismiss these views as racist, a conclusion that does not contribute positively to the debate or control of the disease.

In another article, Ivor Powell reported the composition of the government's new National Aids Council, NAC, as having caused an "uproar" and "experts and activists (*Daily Mail & Guardian*, January 31, 2000) in the fight against Aids are up in arms over the composition of the government's new NAC." The NAC was "riddled with anomalies", among them the representation of "the crucial NGO sector by a little-known American national ... a fundamentalist Christian, not representing South African Aids NGOs." In normal circumstances, such criticism would be seen as legitimate and necessary. In South Africa, it could be read as racist by some leading sections of the black community.

The leading AIDS dissident, Professor Duesberg, was ridiculed by Powell (*Daily Mail & Guardia*, April 3, 2000) as "the self-styled Galileo of the modern age, the man in the centre of the HIV/AIDS controversy" and a man who "aggressively questions the link between HIV/AIDS".

When asked if he were told tomorrow that "you were HIV-positive, what would you do?" Duesberg replied: "I wouldn't be worried about this, not in the least bit."

Duesberg told the *Daily Mail & Guardian* that African Aids and American and European Aids were totally different things, that they had the same name "but that is all they have in common." He blamed the African epidemic on "malnutrition, parasitic infections and poor sanitation." The article concluded:

> Not a single statutory scientific research body in the world -- though several, including South Africa's own, have considered the dissident theory – has given it any credence whatsoever. And at least until President Thabo Mbeki announced his intention to revisit the Aids research, support for Duessberg position was limited among politicians to the right wing, apparently seduced by Duesberg's essentially moralistic counter-hypothesis.

But this fact would escape the memory of those who would like to give Duesberg's views credence. What they would remember is his short answer to the question put directly to him.

Direct and public attack on Mbeki's views by the media is their legitimate right but whether this would have had positive effect on Mbeki and his policies towards HIV/AIDS remained to be seen.

"Startling level of scientific ignorance" is the tittle of Denise Ford's article (*Daily Mail & Guardian*, September 15, 2000). In the article, a medical doctor was quoted as having referred to *Time* magazine's interview in which Mbeki was quoted as saying that "TB (tuberculosis), for example, destroys the immune system" and that "at a certain point if you have TB you will test positive because the immune system is fighting the TB which is destroying it". The medic suggested that Mr Mbeki was "betraying a startling level of scientific ignorance" because HIV "is not a hotchpotch collection of symptoms, as the president seems to allege."

Howard Barrel (*Daily Mail & Guardian*, September 23, 2000) reported a "concern over Mbeki fiasco" with the HIV/AIDS policy. "Deep concern spread through the African National Congress and its parliamentary caucus this week over the corner into which President Thabo Mbeki has led the party and the government over HIV/Aids."

A number of ANC MPs said the fiasco into which Mbeki has led the
party and government over HIV/Aids was the worst failure of political judgement since he succeeded Nelson Mandela in June last year.
Other episodes of poor judgement included Mbeki's approach on the
Zimbabwean crisis, his repeated attacks on white south Africans in
recent months, and what a number of ANC MPs termed his "misman-
agement" of tensions in the tripartite alliance.

Mbeki was not, however, "about to fall. ANC MPs and political analysts believe
he is wounded and will have great difficulty in returning to his earlier political
strength. He is now vulnerable."

Again, in the racially and politically polarised background of South Africa
and AIDS issues, this article would be seen by Mbeki and his supporters as racist
and fishing for opposition to the president's views.

However, some articles were transparently genuine and begged Mbeki to
reverse his views on HIV/AIDS issues. For example an open letter to Mbeki,
signed by three South African scientists (*Daily Mail & Guardian*, May 9, 200)
"working in the field of HIV/AIDS research," reasoned with the President: "While
we appreciate that you as an individual are fully entitled to whatever point of
view you care to hold, as Head of State the kinds of views you are expressing
appear to bind the nation to points of view that we feel are untenable." The
authors expressed how deeply hurt they and those opposed to Mbeki's association with the dissident scientists would feel by using a comparison with the
former apartheid government:

Mr President, consider how the mass of people in this country
would react if you or any other influential politician were to insist
on publicly revisiting the "scientific" justification for the policy of
apartheid by giving a public platform to unrepentant proponents of
the policy. Then consider that your apparent willingness to listen
to and be influenced by people with little or no credibility in the
national or international scientific establishment is as offensive
and causes as much anguish to those of us working to combat

HIV/AIDS as revisiting the justifications for apartheid would to someone who voted your government to power.

An editorial in the *Daily Mail & Guardian* (June 9, 2000) conveyed frustration that Mbeki was "still failing to grasp Aids nettle" and that "his second-guessing of science has set back the fight against Aids and it's time he left science to scientists."

The *Sunday Times* [wsam] of South Africa is one of the leading mainstream weeklies, which had extensive coverage of the HIV/AIDS issues. Laurice Taitz (Sunday Times, May 2, 2000) article debated whether Mbeki was "a wise man" or "a fool?"

The question appeared to have been provided by Mbeki's own citing of "The Fool", a poem by Patrick Pierce, in his speech during the opening of the first meeting of the Presidential AIDS Advisory Panel, PAAP, which included dissident scientists. A highlighted lead under the heading added: "President defends his questioning of the HIV orthodoxy as divided panel gathers to find responses to catastrophe". Mbeki is quoted as saying he was embarrassed to admit that he had then discovered there had been a controversy around HIV/AIDS for a number of years. "I was a bit comforted later when I checked a number of our ministers and found that they were as ignorant as I".

This confession seems to back up other stories that Mbeki's knowledge of the subject, which influenced his views, had been spuriously acquired over the www; and there, it was left to the reader to answer the question for him/herself.

Although the PAAP meetings were closed to the media, someone leaked it to Taitz (*Sunday Times*, May 7, 2000) that the AIDS dissident members of the panel were unhappy with the way the meeting was going. The result was this article entitled: "AIDSs dissidents enraged". "

Although the meeting of 30 scientists and HIV/AIDS specialists took place behind closed doors, the *Sunday Times* has learned that it was less than cordial". Leading dissident scientist, Peter Duesberg, was reported to have shouted in frustration: "It is not fair!" An unidentified delegate had also predicted: "Tomorrow's going to be horrible. Their [the dissidents'] window of opportunity is closing so they're going to be jumping up and down".

In Western democracies, this kind of reporting would be seen as just the media doing their job in an interesting way. If politicians get themselves attracted by the brighter tip of the news iceberg, then they only have themselves to blame if they get wrecked in the process. In South Africa - indeed as elsewhere in Africa - such direct criticism of a leader coming from the white media would be interpreted as racist.

Mainstream Western Media [mwm]

UK/Europe media

The BBC [mm] invited Mbeki to answer questions live from its world-wide audience (Talking Point Special, June 6, 2000). When asked by a listener from Honkong, "Sir, why do you lend credence to theories that the medical community long ago rejected," and was he "concerned that people might fail to take precautions against HIV infection when they hear you question the relationship between HIV and AIDS?", the President avoided the last part of the question altogether and there was no insistence that he answer this vital question. Listeners must have been left wondering about this.

The BBC probably did a better job by providing its listeners with a platform to air their views on HIV/AIDS issues in Africa (December 12, 2000) on the Internet: Hassan B. Sisay, Sierra Leoneans in USA, blamed WHO for using a definition which differs decisively from that used in the West. "Many people are being misdiagnosed and are receiving inappropriate medical attention. This is why President Thabo Mbeki of South Africa has considerable reservations about the epidemiological profile of this killer disease."

Another Sierra Leonean, Henry Williams, in New York, believed that "many people do not still believe that Aids exists because anything could be branded as Aids, especially incurable diseases in the less developed world."

Willy Kisitu, an African in Poland, had a similar opinion saying that "the information we have about Aids in Africa is based mainly on generalised statistics, rumours and predictions."

George Mutua, a Kenyan, asserted that HIV "is a man-made virus that has been let free in Africa either intentionally or unintentionally," therefore there was a need and "moral/human responsibility for the guilty Western countries to acknowledge this fact."

But Sally from UK put the responsibility squarely on Africans: "Africa must learn to take responsibility to reverse the cycle of dependency on the West, in dealing with poverty and the spread of HIV/AIDS."

Chigwe Chapata from Mozambique appeared to agree with Sally, saying that "we will only be able to control the spread of HIV/AIDS when we realise and accept that the problem is here, that it is not from the West and that a solution lies in our own hands."

Christine Parker from USA blamed debt for the epidemic: "The heavy burden of foreign debt has siphoned funds that would otherwise be available for the basic health and social services needed to combat HIV/AIDS." Another Kenyan, John in USA, agreed with Parker, contending that "so long as poverty reigns in Africa, HIV/AIDS will continue to increase."

Frank Gonani, a Malawian in USA, concluded that "with the help of God in prayer, anything is possible. It is a battle we must win!"

If former South African president, Nelson Mandela, had any doubts about HIV being the cause of AIDS, he had kept that view very well to himself, for he is on record as saying he would "accept (BBC, September 29, 2000) the dominant opinion", which is that HIV causes Aids unless proved otherwise. Mandela was diplomatic with Mbeki: "I would like to be very careful because people in our position, when you take a stand, you might find that established principles are undermined, sometimes without scientific backing."

But a statement by the Anglican Church in South Africa was direct, stating that "History will judge the government's inaction over Aids as a crime against humanity on the same scale as apartheid" (BBC, September 20, 2000). The head of the Anglican Church, Archbishop Njongonkulu Ndungani, was quoted as saying "it was becoming clear that the South African Government would not come up with a solution to the Aids problem."

The rest of the mainstream UK/European media followed a remarkably similar approach as the South African mainstream media. In many of these reports, Mbeki often comes across as emphatic, passionate, sometimes ambiguous or even vague or confusing. For example: He was reported to have told the South African legislators that "the programme (*Reuters*, September 20, 2000) of the government in this country is based on this thesis that HIV causes AIDS and everything in the programme says that." But, then, he added in an attempt to clarify: "When you ask the question 'Does HIV cause AIDS?', the question is: 'Does a virus cause a syndrome?' It can't...A virus cannot cause a syndrome. The syndrome is a group of diseases as a result of the immune deficiency, of the acquired immune deficiency syndrome."

An article in *The Times* announced that the South African president was losing popularity fast because of his policies on HIV/AIDS. "Mbeki's star in free-fall as ANC loyalty wanes." Michael Dynes' article (*The Times*, October 21, 2000) reported of an opinion poll in South Africa, which indicated Mbeki's popularity had declined "by 30 per cent." But unemployment was the biggest concern at 76 per cent, while the HIV/AIDS issue was rated at only 13 percent. "This is the first time that more than 10 percent of the population have identified HIV/AIDS as an issue of significant concern." But the politics of HIV/AIDS preoccupied the media, for reasons largely due to the politicians than the media.

Chris McGreal's article (*The Guardian/The Observer*, September 19, 2000) focussed on disagreement between Mbeki and the country's trade union association, Cosatu whose leader "attacked Mbeki for HIV/Aids doubts." Mbeki was reportedly accused by the association of "causing confusion and costing lives by questioning the link between HIV and Aids." "For Cosatu, the link between HIV and Aids is irrefutable and any other approach is unscientific and unfortunately likely to confuse people. As a result, it can undermine the message that all South Africans must take precautions to avoid infection."

If this report is true, it is the view that Mbeki would have to take seriously, for the association is the key to his retaining power come the next election.

Victor Mallet's article (*Financial Times*, February 23, 2000) focused on "anger at Mbeki ahead of Aids conference". The "anger" was over Mbeki's views, the invitation of dissident scientists and the reaction of some leading South African medics and scientists. The president of South Africa's Research Council, Malegapuru Makgoba quoted opinion was that Mbeki had become the champion of discredited scientists who could not find support at home: "I think the dissident group have lost their scientific credibility in the developed world and are looking for a champion in the developing countries. And I think they have struck a fertile environment for pseudo science in South Africa."

But the article also hinted at a suspicion within Mbeki's administration that the pharmaceutical companies selling HIV/AIDS treatment drugs were up to no good. Mallet wrote that Mbeki's spokesman, Parks Mankahlana, had earlier written an article in which he attacked the presidents critics and condemned "the machinations of the profiteering pharmaceutical companies and their propagandists."

The Economist [mwm] (May 25, 200) called readers attention to "South Africa's president and the plague: South Africa's AIDS policy is confused, and President Thabo Mbeki has added to the confusion". The confusion is reported to have come partly from abandonment of a "quack cure" which was previously promoted by the government, and partly from "Mr Mbeki is inclined to take advice from 'dissident' scientists." This was tempered by "However, Mr Mbeki is now making it clear he believes that HIV does indeed cause AIDS", but note that Mbeki had not actually said the virus was the only cause, a point which he and his aides had been trying to reject.

The USA media

The American mainstream media followed the same pattern as South Africa's and Europe's, except that it appeared to be more dramatic and used metaphors more liberally. It was also more blunt in its condemnation of Mebeki' views as is demonstrated by this article from *Slate*'s [mwm] Washington bureau chief who had no doubts about the source and spuriousness of Mbeki's knowledge of HIV/AIDS issues. He also suggested the president had gone crazy: "Thabo Mbeki: Why has South Africa's excellent president gone loco?" was the header. The author, David Plotz (Slate, July 14, 2000), explained why:

Mbeki encountered dissident AIDS research while surfing the Web late one night. He read the scientific papers and now talks confidently about "toxicities" and "the phosphoral relation". He portrays himself as an educated skeptic about AIDS. But his late night Web-trolling, credulity about what he read on line and $10 scientific phrases smack less of skepticism than obsession. The president of South Africa is acting like a nutter.

The message seems clear: Mbeki is crazy; he is airing his limited knowledge – if not ignorance – of medical science; his HIV/AIDS views, policies and actions, are based on spurious information gleaned from the Web. The article says a lot of good things about Mbeki; but all that's in the past, noting: "It's a shame that Mbeki has been diverted by this bizarre AIDS twaddle, because he is normally rational." The author quoted the director of the Program of Intrastate Council at Harvard's Kennedy School, Robert Roberg: "This is very foolish and uncharacteristic of him." Plotz concludes: "If South Africa has become so troubled that even the unflappable Mbeki is coming unhinged, the world should worry."

An article by *Reuters* (CNN, September 20, 2000) advanced the idea that Mbeki had abandoned his original argument and had now submitted to the mainstream's view that HIV causes AIDS. "S. Africa's Mbeki acknowledges assumed link between HIV and AIDS." But this would be misinterpreting the president, as his aides would readily argue that he had never denied the link, except that "the virus cannot be the only cause."

The USA media had the tendency to rely and also expand on what had been reported by the local South African mainstream media. An article by S. Predrag (NBC, May 10, 2000) for example, quoted from an editorial by the *Daily Mail & Guardian*, stating that, "He [Mbeki] seems to have become the international political patron of views on HIV/AIDS which seriously undermine the deployment in this country of the best available science for treating HIV/AIDS and related conditions."

"Severe consequences" of Mbeki's belief and actions were also cited as predictable in this article. "If President Mbeki gives such a public platform to dissident scientists who doubt that HIV causes AIDS, say his local critics, what should an ordinary citizen think causes a disease that is killing almost 6,000 men, women and children daily on this continent?"

Joan Stephenson (*JAMA*, August 2, 2000) had some alarming headings of Biblical proportions: "Apocalypse Now: HIV/AIDS in Africa Exceeds the Experts' Worst Predictions." The use of Black Death as metaphor for AIDS was irresistible to the author of this article who wrote:

> Not since the Black Death devastated medieval Europe has human-kind observed infectious disease deaths on such a massive scale that a country's population has shrunk rather than grown. But the scenario is playing out again in the 21st century, with HIV/AIDS replacing bubonic plague as the killer, according to new data presented here at XIII International AIDS Conference.

The author quoted at length from a study report commissioned by the Agency for International Development/USAIDS which estimated low population growth rate as low as 0.1 per cent for some Southern African countries because of AIDS. Oxford University Professor Roy Anderson was quoted as arguing that "the problem is going to get much worse before it gets better. We don't know how much worse it will get - that depends on what happens from now."

But *Time* magazine's interview with then President Mbeki introduced him by comparing his personality and style of government to that of his predecessor, Nelson Mandela, a comparison which appears to put Mbeki's performance in a very poor light. The magazine argued that, "While Nelson Mandela's office was engagingly open - the man himself homespun to a fault - Mbeki lacks that popular touch." *Time* also suggested that Mbeki had dictatorial and racial tendencies:

> He has reconstructed the presidency around himself into a powerful, impenetrable and, some critic say, (Time, September 11, 2000), disturbingly authoritarian organization. Even his supporters question his apparent backing of dissident scientists views on aids and his passionate - some say quixotic - pursuit of an African renaissance in a continent that continues to tear itself apart through often self-inflicted upheaval. Political opponents charge that when countering

criticism of his strategies and style, Mbeki has begun to play the race card, defining South Africa as a country of two nations - one rich and white, the other poor and black.

TIME: You've been criticised for playing down the link between HIV and AIDS. Where do you now stand on this issue?

Mbeki: Clearly there is such a thing as acquired immune deficiency. The question you have to ask is what produces deficiency. A whole variety of things can cause the immune system to collapse.

TIME: Are you prepared to acknowledge that there is a link between HIV and AIDS?

Mbeki: No, I am saying that you cannot attribute immune deficiency solely and exclusively to the virus.

Fringe/Dissident Media

Mbeki and the political storm he stirred up were the key concerns of the fringe/dissident media: The key adjectival words and phrases used were more or less the opposites of the ones used by the mainstream media. Unlike the mainstream scientists, mainstream organisations and media, dissident scientists and journalists and supporting media saw President Mbeki's views on HIV/AIDS issues as "wise". They saw his actions as overdue intervention from any responsible political leadership.

But they also saw him as the next likely victim of the AIDS establishment and their financial and political backers. They did not only see criticism of his views as ill advised but also as a concerted effort to sideline or get rid of him altogether. Parallel was drawn between what had befallen HIV/AIDS dissidents in the past and what was likely to happen to Mbeki.

Former *Sunday Times* (UK) science correspondent, Neville Hodgkinson, who turned HIV/AIDS dissident in the early 90s and lost his job over it expected that what happened to him would happen to Mbeki because "Aids science is not normal (*New African*, December 2000:28-30) and the criticism of Mbeki, both inside and outside South Africa, could hardly have been more virulent - and ill informed."

Hodgkinson told the *New African* readers in an article headed: "Eight years ago I went through the same experience as Mbeki: An eyewitness account by the former science correspondent of *The Sunday Times.*" The year 2000, he said, saw the birth of a new international sport that became known as "Mbeki-bashing: News papers, broadcast media, doctors and scientists, charities, UN agencies, financial institutions and officials even up to the level of the White House, joined in the fun."

Hodgkinson argued that while on the HIV/AIDS beat in the early 90s he was persuaded by "the evidence" he "discovered" that there was no concrete proof in the widely accepted belief that HIV causes AIDS. He began to write against the concept in a series of articles which led him to Africa. "Out came the big guns" against him and his science editor. These "big guns", he argues, included:

WHO, European Union's Aids Task Force, Britain's Medical Research Council and Chief Medical Officer, representatives of the three major political parties in Britain, the giant drug company Welcome, a group of Nobel prize-winning molecular biologists, numerous science and medical correspondents, the gay press, New Scientist, The lancet, British Medical Journal, leaders of Aids charities, an Oxford professor of poetry, the BBC, and the New York Times among many others.

Those were the forces which he said were marshalled against him and which eventually caused him to lose his job at *The Sunday Times.* These, he argued, were some of the forces that were being marshalled against Mbeki.

A banner with Mbeki's photo on *Rethinking AIDS Website (dm)* reads "Support President Mbeki to find the truth about AIDS" (Nov. 2000). The website refers readers to media articles such as: "Mbeki vs Drugs Inc; ANC Backs Mbeki; Mbeki-Bashing Circus; Replies to Durban Declaration; Act Up SF Under Fire; Time Interview Mbeki; Dissident Symposium Uganda; Newsweek Slammed Maggiore, Newsweek did an interview with *Alive and Well* Christine Maggiore; see also Magiore's reply; Reasons not to Test" and so on and so on. The website appears to have had a new lease of life since Mbeki appeared on the scene.

Editor of *Continuum* [fm] magazine Huw Christie highlighted the successes of the dissident scientists in a report from Johannesburg, titled: "Suspend all HIV testing … Mbeki expert panel recommends." (New African, September 2000:14-16):

> Eminent world scientists from both sides of the Aids debate have been mandated by the Mbeki Aids panel to undertake historic exper-iments to attempt to purify, or isolate, the HIV virus; and also examine the current HIV testing methodologies. In the meantime, the panel wants all HIV testing to be suspended. "It is a worthless distraction," says one panel member.

Christie also had another article, titled, "The great Aids debate that will change the world", (*New African*, May, 2000:8-9), with Mbeki's photo - head and shoulder- right cheek resting on closed fist and looking slightly bemused. The caption read: Mbeki: "I'm amazed at how many scientists are determined that scientific discourse and inquiry should cease."

Huw Christie had quite a run of articles on the HIV/AIDS issue: "Mbeki's 'folly' is grace to the world", is another title of his work (*New African*, June 2000:12-13), a critique of the mainstream media's criticism of Mbeki's views. The subject media in the article include the *International Herald Tribune*, *Washington Times* and the *New York Times*. Their criticism of Mbeki's views appears to be their 'folly'.

An editorial in the (*New African*, November 2000:8-9) ran this header: "Crucify him, crucify him! But in whose interest?" Highlighted under this heading was this: "I think it is dangerous that any of our public representatives and political parties should allow themselves to be used as marketing agents of particular products and companies, including drugs, medicines and pharma-ceuticals companies" - Thabo Mbeki.

The "View from the editor" begins: "Never in the 12-year history of this column, which my former editor Alan Rake kindly named after me, have I stood aside and allowed an outsider to do the talking for me. This month, I am going to do exactly that - because of the seriousness of the occasion and the insight this person brings."

The story this unnamed writer tells is of a worldwide plot against President
Mbeki being secretly conducted through the Internet by people who include
South Africans, some who are not even aware of the serious implication of their
participation:

> I (unnamed) have evidence that the core group are using their
> HIV-Aids Network to get rid of Mbeki as soon as possible, that is, by
> the year 2003 elections. The method is simple: prove that Mbeki is a
> fool for talking to Aids dissidents and buying into their views, and then
> everything he is trying to achieve in terms of an African Renaissance
> is foolish.

But in the South African media, the only indication that Mbeki's views were
having an impact on the views of people living with HIV/AIDS appeared in the
Natal Witness [fm], one of the few South African papers which had given space
to views that the mainstream media would shy away from. An article headed
'Facts about Aids they don't want you to know' (Natal Witness, December 1,
1999) began:

> My name is Penn Xarwalyczha. I write this article so that people may
> make informed decisions. In no way is it my intention to attack the
> many genuine people working in the field of Aids who sincerely believe
> they are helping others. This is an account of a real life event and
> the supporting facts are the words and works of experts and highly
> respected publications. I hope some will be moved to ask the ques-
> tion, "What the hell is going on?"

His story was that because his girl friend was diagnosed as HIV-positive, and he himself expected to be HIV-positive sooner or later, he went
searching for information. He discovered seven "facts" which he did not
know before about HIV-AIDS. Five of them were from the *Sunday Times*
(UK); the remaining two "facts" were attributed to Dr Peter Duesberg and
another dissident scientist.

The *Sunday Times* articles were in fact by Neville Hodgkinson, mentioned earlier. The author said he got all these from the local library, but the articles are also available on Duesberg's Website. His conclusive argument from the "hidden facts" was that "It is rock solid evidence that what we are being told is seriously flawed." He said he had continued to sleep with his girl friend without protection. He reported three negative tests for HIV and by the time of writing he was convinced that the HIV=AIDS=Death formula was false.

Yves Vanderhaeghen of *Natal Witness* had to fight off criticism of the article above with his own: "Shhh . . . not in front of the kids" (*Natal Witness*, December 4, 1999). The article rejected criticism from "the senior deputy vice chancellor of the University of Natal". It asks a question above the heading: "Is it correct to deny people the right to make informed decisions about HIV/AIDS?" Answer:

> On the contrary. All that's 'irresponsible' about the Witness publishing an article on World Aids Day questioning the received wisdom on Aids is that it does not do so more often. The Witness does not consider its readers to be a bunch of zombies who have to be fed an ideologically homogenised diet of 'authorised' news.

A woman living with HIV who used "Angela James" as a pseudonym had an article headed "The voodoo of Aids" (*Natal Witness*, December 7, 1999). Above the heading is this line which seems to cast doubt on predictions made about the HIV/AIDS impact: "To be told you will die in 10 years is a self-fulfilling prophesy." She had also been researching and had ended up confused: "I am not saying 'HIV doesn't cause Aids'. But I am certainly very puzzled by the conviction we all share that it does."

Martin Williams (*Natal Witness*, December 3, 1999) had no doubts about the wisdom of Mbeki's views on HIV and he was publicly in defence of the president. "Mbeki's no Hitler: Awareness lacking on Aids Day" was the header for an article defending President Mbeki from attacks made, among others, by an African American, then in South Africa, who claimed he was HIV-positive and had been kept alive for 20 years by AZT. "Nonsense. HIV was not discovered 20 years ago."

The article labelled as "cranks" those taking advantage of World Aids Day to "accuse President Mbeki of genocide, drawing comparison with Hitler." Mbeki, argues the author, "has very sensibly asked our Health Minister to investigate legitimate concerns about the drug," AZT. "This is not an argument to be settled by peddling untruths or hurling insults at our President".

Williams argued that the HIV/AIDS statistics "do not bear scrutiny." He cited the UNAIDS figures of "33.6 million people are HIV positive, and there were 5.8 million new HIV infections world-wide last year and about 16,000 each day - and more than 95 per cent of these were in developing countries, mostly in Africa." Computer generated figures for KwaZulu, resulted in 200,000 Aids orphans. "Yet, curiously", argued the author, "only 8,000 designated this way are in care."

The article concludes: "In a global context, President Mbeki has played a remarkably important role by asking for AZT to be revisited. Let's hope that by July, when this country hosts the Aids 2000 conference, there will be a more coherent answer."

July 2000 has long come and gone. The debate, though in a fairly reduced tempo, is still going on even now - February 2001. The full report of President Mbeki's HIV/AIDS Panel was received in January 2001; there we leave it.

Impact of HIV/AIDS on Sub-Sahara Africa

An African Problem

Although the first cases of the disease were identified in the United States in 1981 among homosexual men and drug addicts, the disease has since spread all over the world and is now far more endemic in poorer countries, particularly in sub-Sahara Africa, where it is believed to be distributed nearly evenly among sexes and spread mainly through heterosexual intercourse. The latest figures in 2000 (UNAIDS, July 11, 2000) put the total number of sub-Saharan Africans infected with HIV/AIDS at 25.3 millions, including 3.8 millions infections in 2000 alone. Over the same period, "millions of Africans infected in earlier years (UNAIDS, ibid.) began experiencing ill-health, and 2.4 million people at a more advanced stage of infection died of HIV-related illness".

Economically, the future looked extremely bleak for sub-Sahara Africans. As the Aids epidemic kills off or incapacitates almost 20% of the productive age group of 15 - 49 year-olds, national wealth in some parts of Africa was expected to fall "by 15 - 20 percent in the next ten years" (UNAIDS, July 11, 2000). Life expectancy in some African countries had been revised to fall to 35 years instead of 70 for the next ten years. "With AIDS killing off more and more of the workforce group, a vicious circle would develop, whereby poverty increases, thus making it possible for more and more people to get infected with the virus, which then would lead to AIDS and death". The report predicted increasing social instability in Africa.

At first AIDS was not seen as an African problem. But then the HIV strains now commonly found mainly in Africa and which define African AIDS became endemic and HIV/AIDS had now become an African problem. When an American scientist first raised some controversial issues around the science of AIDS, it did not concern Africa. But then President Mbeki's recent sympathy for the views of dissident scientists has now made what was their problem an African problem. The international media could hardly be blamed for focusing on Africa for yet a few more negative reasons.

Media Before Mbeki's Controversy

HIV infections and deaths from AIDS had slowed down in the West, due to education and treatment. Media interest in AIDS had waned considerably. Fewer reporters were turning up at AIDS meetings probably because these conferences were routine with nothing new to reveal and therefore were considered dull. Although HIV/AIDS was spreading fast in Africa and elsewhere in the poorer parts of the world, the Western media could not see this as newsworthy. If the poor in those parts of the world were not dying of AIDS they would be dying of a multitude of other natural or man-made calamities such as earthquakes, floods, famines or war. Reporting from such regions was always difficult, costly and dangerous. Compassion fatigue was also a deterrent.

However, there were occasional in-depth reports of HIV/AIDS in Africa in both mainstream and fringe media before Mbeki's controversy. For example, by the end of 1985 the *New York Times* financed "Laurence Altman's long series of articles on AIDS in Africa (Nelkin, 1995:102) - a rare example of well-funded, detailed, investigative science reporting." Also by the end of 1999, *Village Voice* published "Pulitzer Prize-winning series by Mark Scoofs." (*Village Voice* series, November 1999) under the tittle: "AIDS: The Agony of Africa". These articles informed America of the widespread infections and deaths from HIV/AIDS in Africa. They also informed of the grinding poverty. Schoofs, for instance, noted that:

> Villagers here are so poor that most don't bury their dead in coffins, but merely wrap them in blankets. At one funeral, near the start of Zimbabwe's winter, the grieving family was so destitute that after lowering the body into the grave, they started removing the blanket from the corpse so their children wouldn't go cold.

Schoofs also told of heroes and villains, for example, two brothers: one a national music icon, "Fela (who) didn't believe AIDS existed. But then he died of the disease", and Fela's brother, a medical doctor who "is still trying to convince Fela's fans that HIV is real."

There were a few dissenters within the mainstream media. For example, in 1992 *The Sunday Times* [mm] UK, then science correspondent, Neville

Hodgkinson, who said he "previously reported Aids exclusively from the conventional standpoint - deadly new virus spreading surreptitiously among sexually active people, set to kill millions etc," (New African, December 2000:28-30) began to report the views of dissident scientists. For the next two years Hodgkinson wrote and published in The Sunday Times a series of articles, including many from central Africa. He had concluded that "Aids epidemic" in Africa was "largely an illusion, stemming from major African killer diseases having been mistakenly defined as Aids."

Eventually, however, The Sunday Times returned to the mainstream camp, Hodgkinson lost his job, joined the dissident camp and went on to write a book: "The Failure of Contemporary Science - How a virus That Never Was Deceived the World." Some, among them his former employer, must have thought he was going too far and was being irresponsible. As he himself noted: "The Sunday Times disowned me with a hostile review published long before the book was out."

Meditel (fm/UK) also produced a series of television programmes from 1987 to the late 90s with some of the programmes covering Africa and broadcast by Channel 4 (UK). Like Hodgkinson's, Meditel series also sought to cast doubt on the cause of AIDS, the methods used for HIV tests and the basis for projected statistics for HIV infections and AIDS deaths in Africa. They generally considered HIV/AIDS statistics released by official AIDS organisations as suspect and unreliable.

But their 1998 World Day News report that was "commissioned" by Channel 4 News and was ready for broadcast was rejected by the channel shortly before the broadcast date, (Meditel Web, March 18, 2000). Channel 4, it would appear, had at last decided to return to the mainstream and refused to continue giving platform to the views of dissident scientists. But this act could also have pushed Meditel over to the dissident side.

The only notable African publication that had continued to give voice to AIDS dissidents had been the London-based New African [amd] monthly magazine which constantly questioned UNAIDS figures, HIV test methods and the cause and origin of AIDS. It ran articles with tittles such as: "Are 26 million Africans dying of AIDS?" (December, 1998), "Did Aids really originate from Africa?" (April 1999). "Aids: Let them eat their figures." (September 11, 1999). Consistent titles like these, plus strongly argued editorial opinions in the *New African* against the majority scientists view attracted praise from dissident scientists and fringe/dissident media and sympathisers and bitter criticism from the mainstream scientists and media.

One hard-hitting criticism of the magazine was an article by Neely Tucker, *Free Press* [mm] Foreign Editor (*Detroit Free Press*, August 14, 1999). Tucker directed his criticism at the Editor of the *New African*, Baffour Ankomah, whom he described as "a man with a mission" and that "he wants to convince his readers there is no such thing as AIDS and that millions of Africans aren't dying of it."

Tucker's article titled: "AIDS denial ravages Africa - Conspiracy theories spread with disease", quoted a Senegalese sociologist "who is a director of the UNAIDS programme in central and Southern Africa: "I fear we are moving from private, intimate denial of AIDS to professional denial. People are desperate to find something to blame."

Tucker noted that the magazine was "one of Africa's most respected news magazines" and that its "articles are reprinted in magazines across Africa", implying the serious damage the magazine could do to HIV/AIDS prevention and treatment programmes in Africa.

Tucker also quoted Aulora Stally, then spokeswoman for Southern African AIDS information Dissemination Service, "who watched her brother die of the disease" as saying: "These denials and conspiracy campaigns are almost criminally irresponsible, because they're telling people not to do the one thing that can save their lives -- accept AIDS for what it is, and protect yourself."

Opposing Views

These few examples indicate that, at one end, the mainstream media respects the views expressed by majority of scientists that HIV causes AIDS. It accepts that the disease is endemic and a very serious threat to millions of lives in Africa. It sees those who advance differing opinions from those of the mainstream scientists as irresponsible and dangerous. For the mainstream media, respect for the opinions of the majority scientists has the best chance of success in controlling the spread of the disease.

At the other end the fringe media and dissident journalists, having enter-
tained the idea that the dissident scientists are right in their questioning of the
cause of AIDS, would have little respect if any for the views of the mainstream
or the majority of scientists. In their view, HIV was an innocent virus, which, for
political and economic reasons, was being blamed for the disease. Others, like
the *New African*, saw HIV/AIDS and all the figures of infection and deaths out of
Africa, as just one of the many weapons in the Western armoury for the morale-
bashing of African aspirations. When this political attitude invades, dissident
scientists begin to sound a lot more credible than they really are.

The line between the mainstream scientists and mainstream media on one
end and the dissident scientists and fringe/dissident media on the other was
therefore drawn long before the then South African President entered the fray
and decisively moved the HIV/AIDS debate from the scientific to the political
arena.

Mbeki's News Source of Information

Intense media interest in African AIDS was aroused back in October 1999
when President Mbeki reportedly discovered the dissident scientists' website
and began to wonder aloud about the wisdom of dispensing some retroviral
drugs for treatment of HIV/AIDS infected patients in South Africa. He had also
begun to wonder about the generally accepted view that HIV is the cause of
AIDS. Then he invited well-known dissident scientists to South Africa early in
2000 to join other scientists in discussions about issues that the dissident scientists had been raising over the years.

Mbeki's actions evoked joy in the dissidents' camp and provoked consternation among mainstream scientists. Questions about the cause of AIDS and the
role of the HIV in the whole syndrome; questions about the efficacy, toxicity and
cost of retroviral drugs such as AZT; the reliability of the HIV tests - particularly
in Africa - and the resultant very high statistics of infections and AIDS deaths:
all these became a matter of public concern as they were hotly debated in the
media.

Most of Mbeki's views on HIV/AIDS are contained in two documents he
authored:

"Speech of the President of South Africa, Thabo Mbeki at the Opening Session of the 13th International AIDS Conference, Durban, 9 July, 2000" (Mbeki, 2000);

"S. African President Addresses AIDS in Africa" (*Washington Post*, April 19, 2000). This document, a letter, was "leaked" to the *Washington Post*, which published and distributed it world-wide to the media with this note: "Here is the complete text of the South African President Thabo Mbeki's letter to world leaders on AIDS in Africa. April 3, 2000."

These two documents, plus a number of actions by Mbeki, were the main sources for the issues and actions that had dogged Mbeki's then repeated attempts to clarify his views in the media. It is suggested here that Mbeki's main contentious views and actions, which have proved to be of enduring attraction for the media, are the ones summarised below:

Cause of AIDS: His then widely reported support of the view that "the HIV virus (BBC, April 20, 2000) is not the sole cause of AIDS"; that "AIDS is not a disease", but "a syndrome";

Dissident scientists: The inclusion in Mbeki's panel of advisors on AIDS of some well known "dissident" and "discredited" scientists, "to look into various controversies taking place among the scientists on HIV/AIDS and toxicity of a particular retroviral drug" (Mbeki, April 3, 2000);

Racism: His implied suggestion that there is something racist in a UNAIDS statement that the prevalence of the HIV infection in Southern Africa has increased substantially "in the last five years" by pointing out (Mbeki, ibid.) that the five years "to which Dr. Coll Seck (of UNAIDS) refers coincide closely with the period since our liberation from apartheid, white minority rule in 1994".

Conspiracy theories: His reported support of the "conspiracy theorists who argue that there is a conspiracy between mainstream scientist (Plant, August 4, 1998) on one hand and certain Western governments and multinational pharmaceutical companies on the other, to push the line that HIV is the cause of AIDS and to manufacture expensive drugs for this virus; that these conspirators either sideline or actively work against any support for scientists with alternative theories. "President Thabo Mbeki (BBC, October 6, 2000) has accused the US Central Intelligence Agency (CIA) of working with drugs manufacturers to promote the link between the HIV virus and AIDS to boost profits."

Dangerous and expensive drugs: His reported support of the view that HIV/AIDS treatment drugs, such as "the internationally-used anti-AIDS drug (AFP, 29 October, 2000) AZT" are too dangerous to health and too expensive for South Africa.

Dissidents' cause: His seeming championing of the dissident scientists cause by likening their struggle to historical "heretics that would be burnt at stake" for their differing views:

> People who otherwise would fight very hard (Mbeki, ibid.) to defend the critically important rights of freedom of thought and speech occupy, with regard to the HIV- AIDS issue, the frontline in the campaign of intellectual intimidation and terrorism which argues that the only freedom we have is to agree with what they decree to be established scientific truths. Some agitate these extraordinary propositions with the religious fervour born by a degree of fanaticism, which is truly frightening. The day may not be far off when we will, once again, see books burnt and their authors immolated by fire by those who believe that they have a duty to conduct a holy crusade against infidels.

Uniqueness of African AIDS: His view that the African AIDS epidemic (Mbeki, ibid.) was a "uniquely African catastrophe" which needed "specific and targeted responses to the specifically African incidence of HIV/AIDS", not a "recitation of a catechism that may very well be a core response to the specific manifestation of AIDS in the West."

Dissidents Reassert their Case

Dissident scientists and their supporters saw Mbeki's views as wise and a boost to morale, a timely political lifeline for the long struggle to get their views taken seriously by the scientific establishment. Ten dissident scientists, members of Mbeki's panel, for example, were able to bluntly reassert their case publicly and in a report to President Mbeki (Duesberg et all, 2000):

- AIDS is not contagious although many of the opportunistic manifestations are.
- AIDS is not sexually transmitted.
- AIDS is not caused by HIV.
- The admittedly toxic anti-HIV drugs are killing people.
- The drug induced toxic effects are causing AIDS-defining conditions that cannot be distinguished from AIDS.

The dissidents proceeded to recommend to President Mbeki:

- Devote the bulk of the national and international biomedical and other resources to the eradication and treatment of predominant AIDS-defining diseases in South Africa such as TB, Malaria and enteric infections; the improvement of nutrition; the provision of improved sanitation and clean water.
- Reject completely the use of anti-HIV drugs. These drugs inevitably require significant amounts of compensatory medications and are claimed to produce at best only short-term benefits in seriously sick patients.
- Promote sex education based on the fact that there are many STDs and avoidable unwanted pregnancies.
- Suspend dissemination of the psychologically destructive false message that HIV infection is invariably fatal.
- Suspend HIV testing until its relevance is proved especially in the African context, given the evidence of false positive results in a tropical setting and the fact that most assumptions and predictions about AIDS in Africa are based on HIV-tests.

President Mbeki started to apply some of these recommendations. HIV tests, for example, were suspended.

Reaction of UNAIDS and the Mainstream Scientists

The dissident scientists' recommendations were made just before the main conference in Durban. They were made at the time UNAIDS was issuing a series of press releases on the ever increasing HIV infections and AIDS deaths in Africa. The mainstream scientists and HIV/AIDS activists would take the view that President Mbeki's views were at best a setback and at worst could help the spread of the HIV infections and should be rightly condemned.

Mbeki himself noted that his views on HIV/AIDS were being "condemned by some in our country (Mbeki, 2000, ibid.) and the rest of the world as constituting a criminal abandonment of the fight against HIV/AIDS".

An undated UNAIDS "Background Brief", titled "HIV, AIDS and the reappearance of an old myth", admitted that although "the human immunodeficiency virus (HIV) has been decisively established as the cause of AIDS, a small but vocal group has continued to question the link between HIV and AIDS," that periodically this "results in media attention and generates some renewed public interest in their views." Its reference to South Africa below indicates it was released sometime in early 2000:

> Most recently (UNAIDS, 2000:1), there has been controversy in the South African and International media over the South African government's announcement that it would convene an international panel to re-examine the scientific evidence surrounding AIDS, including evidence regarding the cause and diagnosis of the disease. The debate has also recently resurfaced in other countries.

UNAIDS attributed the origin of the argument that "HIV does not cause AIDS" to Dr. Peter Duesberg whose views "attracted attention in the mainstream press and found resonance with specific groups outside the scientific community."

Open criticism of Mbeki's views were underlined by a signed "declaration by more than 5,000 leading mainstream scientists and doctors", (NBC, July 3, 2000), reasserting that "there is an overwhelming evidence that HIV virus is the cause of AIDS". This document was released to the press a day before the Durban conference, thus sending a clear message to Mbeki the mainstream medical opinion was not on his side and the world had better know; thus implicitly placing Mbeki's views firmly in the dissidents' camp.

Then presidential spokesman, Parks Mankahlana, saw the document as "intolerable" and only "good for the president's dust bin". He wondered how a declaration could be drafted and adopted before the conference. "We have never seen this kind of intolerance (Reuters, July 3, 2000) and we don't want people bringing intolerance to Africa."

CONCLUSION

What was learned?

There were two different periods the study considered: The period before Mbeki's intervention and that between the end of 1999 and 2000. For the first period, it was noted that HIV/AIDS had become an African problem, with infections spreading evenly and faster among the sexes. Even then, media interest was patchy, though some reports were extensive and detailed. Some of the coverage was controversial, though the issues the scientists disagreed on were not yet familiar to the average news consumer in Africa.

The second period was when then President Mbeki made his views known about issues the majority of scientists thought were settled many years back. From then on, what was largely a debate among scientists was given a political twist that almost turned the HIV/AIDS prevention efforts in Africa into a political and media charade throughout 2000.

In terms of news value, Mbeki's sympathy for dissident scientists, plus his own opinions on the subject of HIV/AIDS science, were not expected of a national leader. Such views would be seen as "disrespect for science"; and that precisely was how the mainstream media saw it and interpreted it. For the fringe/dissident media, Mbeki's views and actions were attractive because they were considered brave and wise and that's how they reported it. South Africa's own social, cultural and racial background added to the drama and news value.

But the thesis also proposed that those aspects alone would not have been sufficient reasons for the record attendance of both the media and science researchers at the AIDS conference in Durban. It was argued that the negative reaction of the leading AIDS organisations and the mainstream scientists and the triumphant response from dissident scientists, broadcast over the media, tipped the balance.

The reason why there was so much consternation on one end and jubilation on the other, it was proposed, was due to excessive fears from the mainstream organisations and exaggerated hopes from the dissidents that Mbeki's views would greatly influence the behaviour of Africans in general and South Africans in particular. Mbeki's supposed influence in the region was, for instance, reflected in the BBC "Talking Point Special" programme where the majority of the questions directed at Mbeki concerned the war in the Congo and the land/race conflict in Zimbabwe, and what was he (Mbeki) doing about it?

But judging from the media reports, it would appear that Mbeki's views did not have much impact on the behaviour of South Africans because the majority of other influential individuals and organisations were openly opposed to at least some of his HIV/AIDS views and actions. For instance, the Arch Bishop of the Anglican Church, Nelson Mandela, Desmond Tutu, the majority of South African scientists and medical practitioners, the Trade Union Association, AIDS activists and the mainstream media expressed their fears publicly - a plus for South African democracy.

As for the rest of Africa, a December meeting of the African Development Forum 2000 in Addis Ababa, Ethiopia, in which many presidents spoke, diplomatically ignored President Mbeki's views and continued to hold their meeting as if there was never any question about the cause of AIDS: "AIDS: The Greatest Leadership Challenge" was the theme of the conference.

The Moral imperative for the Media and a Recommendation

What ethical and moral philosophy guided the media in their coverage of HIV/AIDS in Africa during the period under study? Kosoma, would suggest the Western philosophy of journalism largely based on deontological ethics which "requires that ethical issues should not be subjected to the demands of consequence and/or context, but should be based on good intentions that satisfy formal objective conditions and duties." What it means in practice is that the reporter's priority is his/her editor who wants "a good story", which may or may not have considered consequences, be they positive or negative. Consequential considerations, it is suggested, are most likely ignored when news concerns foreigners or remote nations.

This does not, however, mean that journalists and their media are completely free of ethical and moral considerations. In reporting HIV/AIDS issues, ethical and moral considerations must have been difficult to avoid because journalists and their media operate in societies, which expect them to know the difference between right and wrong and should act accordingly.

The attitude of the mainstream media, for instance, had been all along to condemn President Mbeki's views and actions on HIV/AIDS issues presumably because they believed he was wrong and most likely because they believed his views and actions would impact negatively on HIV/AIDS prevention and treatment efforts. Mbeki's later withdrawal from any public debate of HIV/AIDS controversial issues and the government's decision to supply some retroviral drugs to reduce mother to child transmission of HIV, were likely influenced by the mainstream media's pressure on Mbeki.

For those who believe HIV causes AIDS and that retroviral drug treatment is effective - even if it is only in some cases and for limited periods - the mainstream media will have acted responsibly and in the interest of those living with HIV/AIDS and prevention efforts. Those who believe otherwise would label them "irresponsible".

On the other hand, the fringe and dissident media are most likely to have supported Mbeki's views precisely for the same ethical and moral reasons. Since they did not believe in "HIV causes AIDS" theory, giving HIV-positive people admittedly toxic drugs to kill an "innocent virus" would be from their point of view tantamount to poisoning them. Money spent on drugs and prevention of HIV infections would be seen as a waste of badly needed funds to create jobs and reduce poverty - which they believe is a key factor in any "causes" of AIDS.

From this side of the line, Mbeki's later actions would have been seen as submission to the wishes of the HIV/AIDS establishment and pharmaceutical companies; and not in the interest of the poor dying of hunger and of AIDS. This attitude of the fringe media would be praised as "courageous" by dissident scientists and sympathisers and condemned as "irresponsible" by the mainstream.

In this situation, where each side will claim the moral high ground, it would seem reasonable to argue that the majority scientists' view, supported by the mainstream media, prevails and supported by all until proved wrong by an alternative theory. It would also seem unreasonable to insist that the dissident scientists' view, supported by fringe/dissident media, prevails or accorded the same status with the majority's until the mainstream scientists have proved their theory beyond reasonable doubt. This is neither good for democracy nor science nor society - any society. Above all, such arguments are confusing to those who are infected with HIV or dying of AIDS or implementing HIV/AIDS prevention programmes.

The practice of journalism, both in the West and Africa, continues to pretend it is connected to the societies it serves. The reality is that individualistic ethics and morality based on personal judgement of right and wrong predominates. Moemeka and Kasoma, (mentioned earlier) "suggest that African journalists base their journalism ethics on practical approach to morality." They argue that "Utilitarian and situational ethics define a person's action as good only because of their good effect on the community, taking the prevailing conditions into account." In my opinion, there is no good reason why such ethical and moral philosophy based on community's interest should not be universally applicable to any practice of journalism.

Bibliography

Boorstin, Daniel: 1973: *The Image* New York: Athenaeum

Cirino, Robert: 1971: *Don't blame the people* Los Angeles: Diversity Press

Cohen, Stanley & Young, Jock: 1973: *The Manufacture of news. Deviance social problems & the mass media* London: Constable

Ginneken, Jaap van: 1998: *Understanding Global News* London: SAGE

Hartley, John: 1982: *Understanding News* London: Methuen

Kasoma, Francis: 1994: *Journalism Ethics in Africa* Nairobi: African Council for Communication Education.

Moeller, Susan: 1999: *Compassion Fatigue: How the Media sell Disease, Famine, War and Death* London: Routledge

Nelkin, Dorathy: 1995: *Selling Science: How the Press Covers Science and Technology* [Revised Ed.] Washington DC: W.H. Freeman and Company

Tumber, Howard: 1999: *News - A Reader* New York: Oxford University Press

Media Sources

AFP, November 1, 1999: *Safrica-AIDS: S. African doctor takes on Mbeki over anti-AIDS drug* [Internet] AFP, Johannesburg. Available from: <http://www.aegis.com/news/afp/1999/AF991101html>[Accessed 11 January, 2001]

AFP, October 29, 2000: *Mbeki stokes row over anti-AIDS drug* [Internet] AFP, Johannesburg. Available from: <http://www.aegis.com/news/afp/1999/AF991101html>[Accessed 11 January, 2001]

Allen, Anita, March 14, 2000: *The dissident view* [Internet) Daily Mail & Guardian, Johannesburg. Available from:<http://www.mg.co.za/mg/za/achive/2000apr/06apram-news.html>[Accessed January 29, 2001].

Barrel, Howard, June 2, 2000: *Mbeki: One year on* [Internet] Daily Mail & Guardian, Johannesburg. Available from:<http://www.mg.co.za/mg/za/achive/2000apr/06apram-news.html>[Accessed January 29, 2001].

Barrel, Howard, September 23, 2000: *ANC concerned over Mbeki fiasco* [Internet] Daily Mail & Guardian, Johannesburg. Available from:<http://www.mg.co.za/mg/za/achive/2000apr/06apram-news.html>[Accessed January 29, 2001].

BBC News, September 20, 2000: *Mbeki digs in on Aids* [Internet] BBC, 18:40 GMT. London. Available from:<http://www.news.bbc.co.uk/hi/english/world/africa/newsid>[Accessed 10 January, 2001]

BBC News. October 6, 2000: *Mbeki accuses CIA over Aids* [Internet] BBC, 14:50 GMT, London. Available from: <http://www.news.bbc.co.uk/hi/english/world/africa/newsid> [Accessed 12 November, 2000]

BBC News, June 6, 2000: *Thabo Mbeki answers your questions* [Internet] BBC, 14:50 GMT, London. Available from: <http://www.news.bbc.co.uk/hi/english/world/africa/newsid> [Accessed 12 November, 2000]

BBC News, July 14, 2000: *Mandela urges unity against Aids* [Internet] BBC, 14:50 GMT, London. Available from: <http://www.news.bbc.co.uk/hi/english/world/africa/newsid> [Accessed 12 November, 2000]

BBC News, September 14, 2000: *SA Government steps into Aids row* [Internet] BBC, 14:50 GMT, London. Available from: <http://www.news.bbc.co.uk/hi/english/world/africa/newsid> [Accessed 12 November, 2000]

BBC News, September 29, 2000: *Aids: Mandela takes on Mbeki* [Internet] BBC, 14:50 GMT, London. Available from: <http://www.news.bbc.co.uk/hi/english/world/africa/newsid>[Accessed 12 November, 2000]

BBC News, September 20, 2000: *Church enter SA AIDS row* [Internet] BBC, 14:50 GMT, London. Available from: <http://www.news.bbc.co.uk/hi/english/world/africa/newsid> [Accessed 12 November, 2000]

BBC News, September 20, 2000: *Mbeeki digs in on Aids* [Internet] BBC, 14:50 GMT, London. Available from: <http://www.news.bbc.co.uk/hi/english/world/africa/newsid> [Accessed 12 November, 2000]

BBC News, October 6, 2000: *Mbeki accuses CIA over Aids* [Internet] BBC, 14:50 GMT, London. Available from: <http://www.news.bbc.co.uk/hi/english/world/africa/newsid> [Accessed 12 November, 2000]

BBC News, December 12, 2000: *Aids: Too much talk and not enough action?* [Internet] BBC, 14:50 London. Available from: <http://www.news.bbc.co.uk/hi/english/world/africa/newsid> [Accessed 12 November, 2000]

Beresford, Belinda, July 14, 2000: *Lots of talk, not enough action* [Internet] Daily Mail & Guardian, Johannesburg. Available from: >http://www.mg.co.za/mg/za/achive/2000apr/06apram-news.html> [Accessed January 29, 2001].

Beresford, B, Kindra, J & Deane, N, September 15, 2000: *ANC tries to limit fallout* [Internet] Daily Mail & Guardian, Johannesburg. Available from: <http://www.mg.co.za/mg/za/achive/2000apr/06apram-news.html> [Accessed January 29, 2001].

Boyle, Brendan, June 13, 2000: *Mbeki fights frustration* [Internet] Daily Mail & Guardian, Johannesburg. Available from: <http://www.mg.co.za/mg/za/achive/2000apr/06apram-news.html>[Accessed January 29, 2001].

Coste, Phillipe April 21, 2000: *Mbeki's Aids stance leaves scientists in a daze* [Internet] Daily Mail & Guardian, Johannesburg. Available from: <http://www.mg.co.za/mg/za/achive/2000apr/06apram-news.html> [Accessed January 29, 2001].

Daily Mail & Guardian, January 29, 2000: *Results of AZT treatment 'overwhelmingly positive'* [Internet]

Daily Mail & Guardian, Johannesburg. Available from: <http://www.mg.co.za/mg/za/achive/2000apr/06apram-news.html>[Accessed January 29, 2001].

Daily Mail & Guardian, March 14, 2000: *The Majority consensus* [Internet] Daily Mail & Guardian, Johannesburg. Available from: <http://www.mg.co.za/mg/za/achive/2000apr/06apram-news.html> [Accessed January 29, 2001].

Daily Mail & Guardian, March 14, 2000: *Mixed HIV/Aids messages from government* [Internet]

Daily Mail & Guardian, Johannesburg. Available from: <http://www.mg.co.za/mg/za/achive/2000apr/06apram-news.html>[Accessed January 29, 2001].

Daily Mail & Guardian, April 3, 2000: *A former 'dissident' airs his views* [Internet]

Daily Mail & Guardian, Johannesburg. Available from: <http://www.mg.co.za/mg/za/achive/2000apr/06apram-news.html>[Accessed January 29, 2001].

Daily Mail & Guardian, April 19, 2000: *Mbeki pushes case of Aids 'dissidents'* [Internet]

Daily Mail & Guardian, Johannesburg. Available from: <http://www.mg.co.za/mg/za/achive/2000apr/06apram-news.html> [Accessed January 29, 2001].

Daily Mail & Guardian April 6, 2000: *Five die during Aids trials* [Internet]

Daily Mail & Guardian, Johannesburg. Available from:<http://www.mg.co.za/mg/za/achive/2000apr/06apram-news.html>[Accessed January 29, 2001].

Daily Mail & Guardian, June 9, 2000: *Still failing to grasp Aids nettle* [Internet]

Daily Mail & Guardian, Johannesburg. Available from: <http://www.mg.co.za/mg/za/achive/2000apr/06apram-news.html> [Accessed January 29, 2001].

Daily Mail & Guardian, January 29, 2000: *Results of AZT treatment 'overwhelmingly positive'* [Internet]

Daily Mail & Guardian, Johannesburg. Available from: <http://www.mg.co.za/mg/za/achive/2000apr/06apram-news.html> [Accessed January 29, 2001].

Dickson, Peter, February 7, 2000: *Aids activists set up watchdog* [Internet]

Daily Mail & Guardian, Johannesburg. Available from: <http://www.mg.co.za/mg/za/achive/2000apr/06apram-news.html>[Accessed January 29, 2001].

Duesberg, Peter et all May 7, 2000: *Minority Report and Recommendations of S.A. AIDS Panel* [Internet] AidsMyth Dissident News, Durban. Available from: <http://www.aidsmyth.com/news.htm>[Accessed 11 January, 2001]

Dynes, Michael, October 21, 2000: *Mbeki star in freefall as ANC loyalty wanes* [Internet] THE TIMES, London. Available from:<http://www.thetimes.co.uk/article/0,,18-22689,00.html> [Accessed 30 January, 2001]

Economist, May 25, 2000: *South Africa's president and the plague* [Internet] Economist, London. Available from: <http://www.economist.com/displayStory.cfm?Story_ID=334597> [Accessed 15 January, 2001]

Ford, Denise, September 15, 2000: *A startling level of scientific ignorance* [Internet] Daily Mail & Guardian, Johannesburg. Available from:<http://www.mg.co.za/mg/za/achive/2000apr/06apram-news.html>[Accessed January 29, 2001].

Ka-Mankazana, Mxolisi, March 14, 2000: *'Irrational Aids debate rides rough-shod over patients'* [Internet] Daily Mail & Guardian, Johannesburg. Available from: <http://www.mg.co.za/mg/za/achive/2000apr/06apram-news.html>[Accessed January 29, 2001].

Kindra, J & Daniels, G, September 8, 2000: *Cosatu slams govt Aids policy* [Internet] Daily Mail & Guardian, Johannesburg. Available from: <http://www.mg.co.za/mg/za/achive/2000apr/06apram-news.html> [Accessed January 29, 2001].

Le Page, David, March 14, 2000: *Politicians unwilling to stubborn science* [Internet) Daily Mail & Guardian, Johannesburg. Available from: <http://www.mg.co.za/mg/za/achive/2000apr/06apram-news.html>[Accessed January 29, 2001].

Magardie, Khadija, June 9, 2000: *Aids slashes expectancy* [Internet] Daily Mail & Guardian, Johannesburg. Available from: <http://www.mg.co.za/mg/za/achive/2000apr/06apram-news.html>

Mallet, Victor, March 23, 2000: *Anger at Mbeki ahead of Aids conference* [Internet] Financial Times, London.

McGreal, Chris, September 19, 2000: *Mbeki attacked for HIV/AIDS doubts* [Internet] The Guardian/The Observer, London. Available from: <http://www.guardianunlimited.co.uk/international/story>

Mbeki, Thabo, April 3, 2000: *Letter to World Leaders on Aids in Africa* [Internet] The Memory Hole, Available from: <http://www.blancmange.net/tmh/mbeki.shtml> [Accessed 19 January, 2001]

McKie, R. & Beresford, D, May 8, 2000: *Africa's Aids fate hangs in a balance* [Internet) Daily Mail & Guardian, Johannesburg. Available from: <http://www.mg.co.za/mg/za/achive/2000apr/06apram-news.html>[Accessed January 29, 2001].

Nicodemus, Aaron, July 19, 2000: *Aids policy is a disaster* [Internet) Daily Mail & Guardian, Johannesburg. Available from: <http://www.mg.co.za/mg/za/achive/2000apr/06apram-news.html> [Accessed January 29, 2001],

Plant, Aaron, 1998: *Dissident Scientists and Government Conspiracy: A Look at Alternative AIDS Theories* [Internet] InSite, USA. Available from: <http://www.hivinsite.eucsf.edu/social'spotlight/2098.3d50.html> [Accessed 19 January, 2001]

Plotz, David, July 14, 2000: *Thabo Mbeki: Why has South Africa's excellent president gone loco?* [Internet] Slate, Washington. Available from:< http://www.slate.msn.com/Assessment/00-07-14/Assessment.asp>[Accessed 11 January, 2001]

Powell, Ivor, January 31, 2000: *Uproar over Aids council* [Internet] Daily Mail & Guardian, Johannesburg. Available from: <http://www.mg.co.za/mg/za/achive/2000apr/06apram-news.html>[Accessed January 29, 2001].

Powell, Ivor, April 3, 2000: *The self-styled Galileo of the modern age*[Internet] Daily Mail & Guardian, Johannesburg. Available from: <http://www.mg.co.za/ mg/za/achive/2000apr/06apram-news.html>[Accessed January 29, 2001].

Predrag, S, May 10, 2000: *AIDS debate rages in South Africa* [Internet] NBC, USA. Available from: <http://www.msnbc.com/news/405826.asp>

Reuters, July 3, 2000: *South Africa slams AIDS declaration, Too soon to say whether HIV is cause of AIDS, Mbeki says* [Internet] MSNBC, US. Available from:<http://www.msnbc/news/428653.asp> [Accessed 6 November, 2000]

Reuters, September 20, 2000: *S. Africa's Mbeki acknowledges assumed link between HIV and AIDS* [Internet] CNN, Atlanta. Available from: <http://europe. cnn.com/2000/WORLD/africa/09/20/safrica.mbeki.reut/> [Accessed 11 January, 2001]

Roberts, Bronwen, April 6, 2000: *White media vilify black leaders - ANC* [Internet] Mail & Guardian, Johannesburg. Available from: <http://www.mg.co.za/mg/za/ achive/2000apr/06apram-news.html> [Accessed January 29, 2001].

Rybick, E. Williamson, A. & Morris, L May 9, 2000: *Open letter to President Mbeki* [Internet] Mail & Guardian Johannesburg. Available from:<http://www.mg.co. za/mg/za/achive/2000apr/06apram-news.html> [Accessed January 29, 2001].

Science, December 9, 1994: *The Duesberg Phenomenon Science*. Vol. 26, USA

Stephenson, Joan, August 2, 2000: *Apocalypse Now: HIV/AIDS in Africa Exceeds the Experts's Worst Predictions* [Internet] JAMA, USA. Available from:<http:// jama.ama-assn.org/issues/v284n5/full/jmn0802-5.html>[Accessed Januar 4, 2001]

Swindells, Steve, April 19, 2000: *Media racism inquiry prepares report* [Internet] Mail & Guardian Johannesburg. Available from:<http://www.mg.co.za/mg/za/ achive/2000apr/06apram-news.html> [Accessed January 29, 2001].

Taitz, Laurice, May 7, 2000: *Mbeki: Wise man or fool?* [Internet] Sunday Times, Johannesburg. Available from: <http://www.suntimes.co.za/2000/05/07/ politics/pol01.htm> [Accessed 15 January, 2001]

Taitz, Laurice, May 7, 2000: *AIDS dissidents enraged* [Internet] Sunday Times, Johannesburg. Available from:<http://www.suntimes.co.za/2000/05/07/ politics/pol01.htm> [Accessed 15 January, 2001]

Taitz, Laurice., May 19, 2000: *The strange debate on the science of AIDS* [Internet] Sunday Times, Johannesburg. Available from: <http://www.suntimes.co.za/2000/05/07/politics/pol01.htm> [Accessed 15 January, 2001]

TIME, September 11, 2000: *Mbeki - Africa's challenge* [Internet] TIME, Europe. Available from: <http://www.time.com/time/europe/magazine/2000/01911/Mbeki.html> [accessed15 January, 2000]

Trengrove-Jones, Timothy, April 3, 2000: *Disarray in SA's HIV'Aids policy* [Internet] Mail & Guardian Johannesburg. Available from: <http://www.mg.co.za/mg/za/achive/2000apr/06apram-news.html> [Accessed January 29, 2001].

UNAIDS, 2000: *HIV, AIDS and the reappearance of an old myth* [Internet UNAIDS Special , Features, Geneva. Available from: <http://www.unaids.org/special/>[Accessed 11 December 2000]